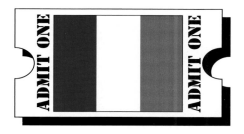

The Eiffel
Tower In Paris
Was Built For
The Universal
Exposition
In 1889.

FACES AND PLACES

FRANCE

BY KATHRYN STEVENS

THE CHILD'S WORLD®, INC.

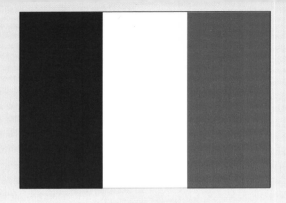

GRAPHIC DESIGN AND PRODUCTION
Robert E. Bonaker / Graphic Design & Consulting Co.

PHOTO RESEARCH
James R. Rothaus / James R. Rothaus & Associates

COVER PHOTO
A French boy wearing a beret
©Nik Wheeler/CORBIS

Library of Congress Cataloging-in-Publication Data
Stevens, Kathryn, 1954–
France / by Kathryn Stevens.
p. cm.
Includes index.
Summary: Describes the geography, history, people,
and customs of France.
ISBN 1-56766-714-7 (lib. bdg. : alk. paper)

1. France — Juvenile literature.
[1. France.] I. Title

DC17 .S74 2000   99-042408
944 21 — dc21

Table of Contents

If you could view Earth from outer space, you would see large land areas called **continents.** One land area is larger than the others. Most of it is taken up by the continent of Asia, but the western end is called Europe. France is near the western edge of Europe.

Western Hemisphere

Eastern Hemisphere

France (white) Is In Both Hemispheres. U.S.A. (green) Is In The West

France is sometimes called "the **Hexagon**" because it has six sides. On three sides it lies

The World Shown Flat

next to water—the English Channel, the Atlantic Ocean, and the Mediterranean Sea. On the other three sides, it lies next to other countries— Spain, Italy, Switzerland, Germany, Belgium, and tiny Luxembourg.

Arctic Ocean

NORTH AMERICA

United States of America

Atlantic Ocean

Pacific Ocean

SOUTH AMERICA

ASIA

EUROPE
France

AFRICA

Indian Ocean

Pacific Ocean

AUSTRALIA

ANTARCTICA

ENGLAND
(UNITED KINGDOM)

Strait of Dover

BELGIUM

GERMANY

English Channel

LUXEMBOURG

FRANCE

SWITZERLAND

Atlantic
Ocean

ITALY

Bay of Biscay

Gulf of Lion

CORSICA
(FRANCE)

SPAIN

Mediterranean
Sea

The Landscape
Surrounding
Biot

NORMANDY
PROVINCE
★ Paris

● Biot
MASSIF
CENTRAL
ALPS

PYRENEES

The Land

The Twin Mountains Castor And Pollux In The French Alps

©John Noble/CORBIS

France is a land of contrasts. Most of France has broad plains, low hills, and wide valleys and basins. These regions have rich soils for growing crops. The Massif Central (mass-EEF sen-TRAHL) in southern France is a rugged, raised "table" of rock called a **plateau**.

Southern and eastern France have two famous mountain ranges. The rocky Pyrenees (PIH-ren-eez) form a natural wall between France and Spain. The scenic, snow-capped Alps run through France, Germany, Austria, Switzerland, and Italy.

©Roger Ressmeyer/CORBIS

Les Falaises Chalk Cliffs Along The Normandy Province Coastline

Long ago, most of France was forested. Animals such as deer, wild boars, and even wolves roamed the woods. Gradually, people turned almost all the forests into farmland. Most of the wild animals died out.

Fallow Deer Near Chamonix

©Tim Thompson/CORBIS

A Wild Boar Lying In A Bed Of Mud

©Clive Druett; Papilio/CORBIS

More recently, parks have been set aside to preserve some of France's natural environment. Today, about one-quarter of France is wooded, much of it in the parks and mountains. Common types of trees include pine, ash, beech, cypress, olive, and oak.

©Michael Busselle/CORBIS

★ Paris

Chamonix•

ARIÈGE
REGION

Autumn
Foliage In
The Ariège
Region

The
Acqueduct
Roquefavour
Near
Ventabren

Lascaux

Ventabren

France has a long, complex history. The early humans who lived there more than 30,000 years ago left behind stone tools and beautiful cave paintings. By about 2,500 years ago, France (then called "Gaul") was ruled by tribes of Celts (KELTS). In 59 B.C., Gaul was conquered by Julius Caesar and the Roman Empire. About 500 years later, Germanic tribes called Franks took over. Other peoples, from Arabs to Vikings, also tried to conquer France.

©Bettmann/CORBIS

A Portrait Of Napoleon Bonaparte In 1813

France was ruled by one king after another. The kings were very rich while the common people were very poor. In the French Revolution of 1789, King Louis and Queen Marie Antoinette were overthrown. In 1799, a brilliant general named Napoleon Bonaparte seized power. After trying to conquer Europe, Napoleon was defeated at the Battle of Waterloo in 1815.

An Ancient Cave Painting Of Cattle Near Lascaux

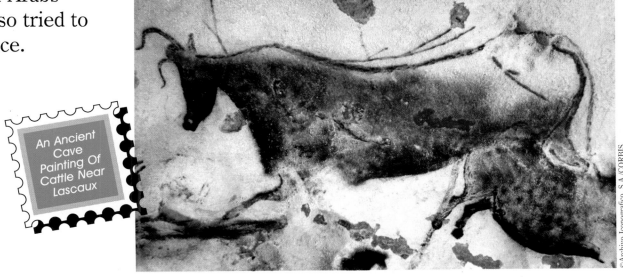

©Archivo Iconografico, S.A./CORBIS

French Resistance Forces Defending A Paris Street During WWII

©Bettmann/CORBIS

In the 1900s, France was at the center of European events. World War I (1914–1918) killed 1.5 million French soldiers and destroyed many towns. During World War II (1939–1945), Adolph Hitler and Germany's Nazi army took over France. A secret "Resistance" movement kept fighting the invaders. Near the end of the war, Allied armies freed France.

Today France is part of the European Union, a group of 15 European nations. These nations have joined together as business and political partners. The European Union even has its own form of money, called the *euro*.

©CORBIS

American Troops Fighting Near Verdun During World War I

14

★ Paris • Verdun

©Paul Almasy/CORBIS

A Gypsy Couple In The French Countryside

★ Paris

PROVENCE-ALPES CÔTE-D'AZUR

F rance's population is a complex mixture. People who invaded or fought over France left their traces in the population. Other newcomers, or **immigrants**, moved to France from nearby countries such as Italy and Spain. More recently, immigrants have come from former **colonies**—distant lands once ruled by France. France once ruled colonies in Africa, Asia, and other regions.

Over three-quarters of France's people consider themselves to be Roman Catholics. A much smaller number follow Islamic, Protestant, Jewish, or other religious beliefs. Most Arab immigrants from North Africa and the Middle East follow the Islamic faith.

A Man Wearing A French Beret In Provence-Alpes Côte d'Azur

©Catherine Karnow/CORBIS

A Restaurant Staff Toasting Wine In Paris

©Charles O'Rear/CORBIS

**City Life
And
Country
Life**

ADMIT ONE

ADMIT ONE

An Old Stone House In The Country Near Vouvray-sur-Loir

Over three-quarters of France's people live in cities. One-sixth live in and around the famous city of Paris. Paris is especially well known for its art, literature, music, fashion, and magnificent buildings. Many city-dwellers live in apartments. Some apartments are in new high-rise buildings, and others are in centuries-old buildings.

Less than one-quarter of France's people still live in the country. Most of them live on farms or in villages. Some farms and villages look as though they have changed little for hundreds of years. Others are more modern.

Apartment Houses In Casinca, Corsica

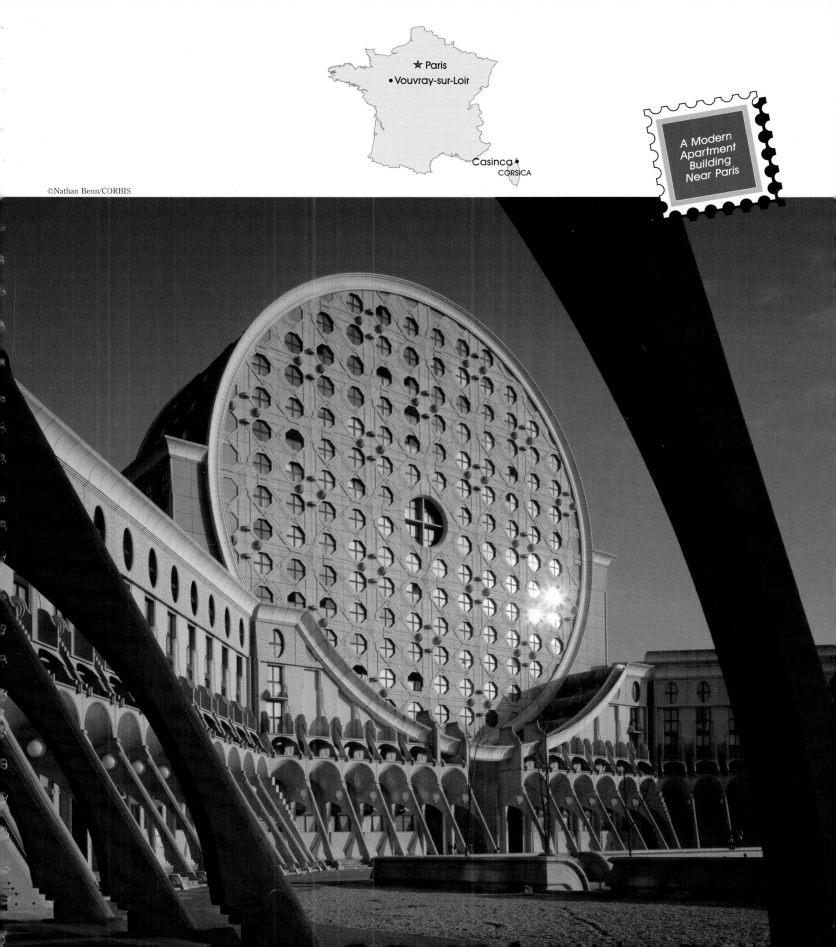

★ Paris

• Vouvray-sur-Loir

Casinca •
CORSICA

A Modern
Apartment
Building
Near Paris

A High School English Language Class In Paris

★ Paris

• Vaucluse

©Owen Franken/CORBIS

All French children must attend school from age 6 to 16. Some begin as early as age 2. From age 6 to 11, the children go to primary schools, learning reading, writing, and other basic skills. Next they attend secondary schools to learn more advanced subjects. After passing a difficult test, some students go on to universities.

Schoolboys Doing Their Lessons On An Outdoor Stairway In Paris

©Owen Franken/CORBIS

France's official language, French, is known around the world. Some people in France speak local variations of French, called **dialects.** Others speak languages such as Alsatian, Breton, or Basque. French dialects and other languages are most common near France's borders. There the languages and customs of the different countries overlap.

A Sign For Honey At A Store In Vaucluse

J'AIME LE MIEL c'est bon

hum!

©Tom Bean/CORBIS

Harvesters Picking Wine Grapes In Banyuls

©Peter Turnley/CORBIS

French people work at a wide range of jobs. Many work in offices, shops, or open-air markets. Others work in factories that produce machinery, metals, foods, and other products sold around the world. French airplanes and cars are especially well-known products.

A Worker At A Steel Factory In Firminy

©Marc Garanger/CORBIS

A much smaller number of people still make a living off the land. Some work as farmers, growing wheat, sugar beets, grapes, potatoes, barley, apples, and other plants. Farmers also raise cattle, chickens, and pigs. Many foods are sold at local markets, and many are sold to other countries.

©Paul Almasy/CORBIS

Firminy

Nice

Banyuls

A Carpenter At Work In Nice

A Chef
Cooking
Mushrooms At
A Cooking
School In
Paris

Paris ★ CHAMPAGNE
REGION

BURGANDY
REGION

● Bordeaux
● Roquefort

CORSICA

French cooking, or **cuisine** (kwih-ZEEN), is famous worldwide. French cooks make a wide variety of breads, pastries, cheeses, soups, meats, and sauces. Breads are popular, and so are pastries such as flaky *croissants* (krwah-SANCE). Different regions have their own local food specialties. World-famous Roquefort cheese, for example, comes from a village in southern France. There it is made and aged in the village's deep caves.

France is also known for its wines, which are sold all over the world. The regions of France called Burgundy, Champagne, and Bordeaux all have types of wine named after them. Grapes are grown and made into wine at places called **vineyards.**

Roquefort Cheese In The Cave Where It Is Made

©Adam Woolfitt/CORBIS

A Baker Baking Pastries On Corsica

©Adam Woolfitt/CORBIS

In the cities, especially Paris, people like to go to concerts, theaters, museums, movies, and fine restaurants. Sidewalk restaurants called *cafés* (kah-FAYS) are popular in both large cities and smaller towns. People sit at the cafés drinking coffee, eating, reading, playing cards, and visiting with friends.

French people like outdoor sports, too. Bicycle racing, soccer, rugby, and tennis are very popular. Many people still enjoy *boules,* an outdoor bowling game. Along the beautiful beaches of the French Riviera, people swim in the ocean and relax in the sunshine. In the mountains, they ski and hike.

French people celebrate a number of holidays. Children receive gifts on Christmas (called "Noël") and Easter ("Pâques," or "PAHK"). May 8 is Victory Day, which celebrates the end of World War II. July 14 is the national holiday, Bastille Day. Bastille Day celebrates the "storming" of the Bastille prison in 1789—one of the best-known events of the French Revolution.

France is known worldwide for its rich culture and heritage. If you visit France, you will find lots of beautiful things to see, from museums to scenic countryside. You will also find plenty of interesting things to do, from hiking to tasting the country's fine foods. You will never be bored in France!

Teams From France (Blue) And Brazil Playing Soccer

Giverny • ★ Paris

©Catherine Karnow/CORBIS

Area
About 210,000 square miles (544,000 square kilometers)—a little larger than Texas.

Population
About 59 million people.

Capital City
Paris, sometimes called the "City of Light."

Other Important Cities
Lyon (lee-OHN), Marseille (mar-SAY), Bordeaux (bor-DOH), Toulouse (too-LOOS), and Nice (NEESE).

Important Rivers
The Rhine, Loire, Seine, Rhône, and Garonne.

Money
The franc (FRAHNK). One franc is made up of 100 centimes (SAHN-teem).

National Flag
A flag with one blue stripe, one white stripe, and one red stripe. White was the color used by France's Bourbon family of kings. Red and blue stripes, which stood for Paris, were added when the Bourbon king was overthrown.

National Song
"La Marseillaise," or "The Song of Marseille."

Head of Government
The president of France.

The Gardens
Of Painter
Claude
Monet
At Giverny

France Trivia

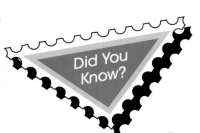

Did You Know?

France is now linked to England by an underwater tunnel. Trains carry cars and people through this English Channel Tunnel, or "Chunnel," which is 32 miles (50 kilometers) long.

The Louvre (LOO-vrh) in Paris, once an enormous palace, is now the world's best-known art museum. The Louvre displays some 30,000 works of art, including the famous painting called the Mona Lisa.

Paris's famous Eiffel Tower was built for the Paris Exposition of 1889. Made of iron, it is 984 feet (300 meters) high! On a clear day, you can see for 50 miles from the top.

Versailles (vare-SYE) is the largest palace in the world. It was built in the 1600s by more than 30,000 craftspeople.

Some of France's flowers are grown especially for their scent. The flowers are taken to factories and turned into expensive perfumes.

French high-speed trains travel at 160 miles (260 kilometers) an hour!

How Do You Say?

	FRENCH	*HOW TO SAY IT*
Hello	Bonjour	bohn-ZHOOR
Good-bye	Au revoir	oh reh-VWAHR
Please	Si'l vous plait	seel voo PLAY
Thank You	Merci	mehr-SEE
One	Un	UHN
Two	Deux	DEUH
Three	Trois	TRWAH
Yes	Oui	WEE
No	Non	NOHN

colonies (KOL-uh-neez)
Colonies are lands ruled by a faraway country. France once ruled colonies in Africa, Asia, North America, and other parts of the world.

continents (KON-tin-ents)
Continents are large land areas mostly surrounded by water. Europe is the eastern part of an enormous continent that also includes Asia.

cuisine (kwih-ZEEN)
Cuisine is a style or way of cooking. French cuisine is famous all over the world.

dialect (DY-uh-lekt)
A dialect is a local version of a language. Some people in France speak dialects of the French language.

hexagon (HEX-uh-gon)
A hexagon is a shape with six sides. People sometimes call France "the Hexagon" because of its shape.

immigrants (IH-mih-grents)
Immigrants are people who move to a country from somewhere else. Many of France's recent immigrants have come from Africa.

plateau (pla-TOH)
A plateau is a broad "table" of land higher than the land around it. Southern and eastern France have some high plateaus.

vineyards (VIN-yerd)
A vineyard is a place in which grapes are grown and turned into wine. France has some of the best-known vineyards in the world.

Index

Web Sites

Learn more about France:
http://www.france.com

Learn more about the Eiffel Tower:
http://www.tour-eiffel.fr/indexuk.html

Take a fun virtual trip around France:
http://www.zipzapfrance.com/anglais/boussole.html

Learn how to make croissants:
http://breadrecipe.com/az/croissants.asp

Learn more words in French:
http://www.travlang.com/languages/
(Then be sure to click on the word "French.")

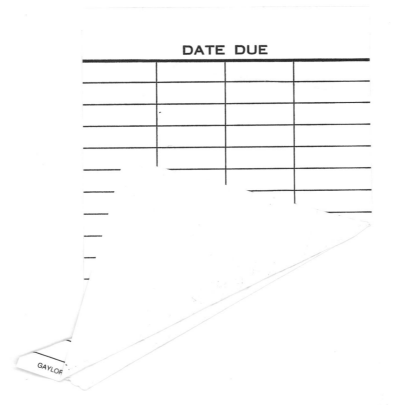

DATE DUE

GAYLORD